JOHN ARDEN

'Roger Mayne

JOHN ARDEN

by

GLENDA LEEMING

Edited by Ian Scott-Kilvert

PUBLISHED FOR
THE BRITISH COUNCIL
BY LONGMAN GROUP LTD

LONGMAN GROUP LTD
Longman House, Burnt Mill, Harlow, Essex

*Associated companies, branches and
representatives throughout the world*

First published 1974
© Glenda Leeming 1974

*Printed in Scotland by
Her Majesty's Stationery Office at HMSO Press, Edinburgh*

ISBN 0 582 01240 6

JOHN ARDEN

I

UNQUESTIONABLY one of the major British playwrights of his generation, John Arden is also one of the most difficult to comprehend: his importance has not led to great popular success, none of his plays has been filmed, and it is not easy, at a first viewing, to grasp the exact intention of his works—although this does not mean that he writes about 'failure of communication'. Yet after renewed critical rebuffs and interludes of minor experimental work—a Nativity play, a mime—again and again Arden produces fascinating large-scale dramas. Far from bending to commercial demands, these have usually gone directly against the theatrical fashions of their time: Arden grows more, not less, uncompromising as he goes on writing.

As the North of England background of many of his plays suggests, John Arden was born in Yorkshire, in Barnsley in 1930. Educated first at a local primary school, but sent to a boarding school to escape the bombs during the war, he attended Sedbergh, a public school 'with less nonsense about it than most of the public schools I've heard about', according to Arden. Although his early-established ambition was to be a writer, he considered that taking a degree in English literature was more likely to dry up his creativity than cultivate it, and so he studied architecture for three years at Cambridge University and for a further two years at Edinburgh Art College. In more ways than one Arden is the most traditionally formed dramatist of his contemporaries; not only is he the only one to have had a university education, but his early ambitions meant that he had a long writing apprenticeship, from schoolboy juvenilia (medieval epic dramas) to less unwieldy, more practicable pieces, such as the Victorian comedy *All Fall Down*, never published but performed by his fellow students at Edinburgh.

Arden only practised his chosen profession for two years, in a London office. During this time, one of his plays, *The Life of Man*, a stark sea story orchestrated with ballads and oceanic sound effects, won a prize in a BBC Northern Region competition, and attracted the attention of George Devine, who decided that the newly launched English Stage Company at the Royal Court should perform Arden's *The Waters of Babylon* (1957).[1] It is hard to overestimate the importance of the Royal Court in supporting the New Wave of British drama in the 1950s. Many new, unorthodox writers, whose plays were unlikely to attract a big enough audience to finance full-scale productions, gained the opportunity of performance in the Royal Court's economic Sunday night 'Productions without Décor'— *The Waters of Babylon* was one of these. It was when the Royal Court commissioned another play from him that Arden left the architects' office to write full time. This confidence was justified, for, after the production of *Serjeant Musgrave's Dance* (1959, probably still his best known play, later performed by amateur and professional companies all over the country, and studied as an examination text in schools), he received a Playwriting Fellowship at Bristol University, and was to be offered various commissions after that. It reveals much about Arden's concept of the dramatist's role that, as well as touching the two poles of vital dramatic force—in his probing socially oriented subjects and in the traditional form of beautiful and arresting dramatic verse—he accepts even the most limited and limiting of commissions for small-scale works. Often these involve a close relationship with the performing company: thus, Arden's wife and co-author, actress Margaretta D'Arcy, directed the Nativity play written for villagers in Somerset, where they were then living. When the Ardens moved to Kirbymoorside, a North Yorkshire village, Margaretta D'Arcy devised a more exploratory involvement in the local community in the shape of a thirty-day, unofficial, theatrically-biased festival—no suitable short label exists. A film was made, small fringe theatre troupes came and went, putting on modern and improvised plays, and there was dancing into the night at the Ardens' cottage. Arden cautiously managed this festival, feeling all the time 'that I was not built for this kind of responsibility', and both Ardens were

[1] Dates given in the text are of first production, not publication.

4

careful not to claim any ulterior, educative aims beyond providing enjoyment for participants and local audience. This was 1963, and a placid and in many ways a satisfying way of life was open to the Ardens: they had their place in the Yorkshire village, and their work enjoyed occasional noteworthy productions—the National Theatre Company was at this time putting on *The Workhouse Donkey*, and this was to be followed the next year by *Armstrong's Last Goodnight*, establishing for Arden a reputation that led to the commissioning of *Left-Handed Liberty* in 1965. But this was to be the last prestige production for some years, for the Ardens turned their energies more and more to exerting political effectiveness through their plays. Spending long periods in Ireland (Margaretta D'Arcy's birthplace), the Ardens and their four sons moved to Muswell Hill, a respectable, unfashionable part of North London, and their plays began to reflect the very pointed personal appeals of actors to audience characteristic of the experimental theatre groups with which they sometimes worked. The longest of these plays, *The Hero Rises Up*, is unusual, for instance, in that its dramatic force does not go to create the self-contained, internally coherent (if complex) plot typical of Arden's plays, but is aimed always at the audience, making a series of different effects, by tableaux, exposition, ballads and scenes with commentaries.

Originally inclined to pacifism—he was for some time chairman of the pacifist newspaper *Peace News*—Arden came during his London period to adopt more militant principles, especially after travelling to India. Much of his most recent play, *The Island of the Mighty* (1972), draws indirect inspiration from this visit. The translation of current events into self-contained historical events so that they can be seen whole also shaped *Armstrong's Last Goodnight*, which was influenced by the crisis in the Congo and Conor Cruise O'Brien's book *To Katanga and Back* (1962); similarly, the Colonial War in *Serjeant Musgrave's Dance* was based on the unrest in Cyprus at the time of its writing. The autobiographical 'dream' play, *The Bagman*, marks a turning point here, for though the play seems to conclude that Arden's writing was only adapted to indirect social satire, his preface stresses that he has already discarded that view. Indeed, the war the Ardens declared in *Harold Muggins is a Martyr* (1969) upon the financial pressures and authoritarian structures that affect the man in the street, erupted in their own lives when they quarrelled with the managements of *The Hero Rises Up* and *The Island of the Mighty*. In both cases, the administrative and economic requirements of the plays' backers collided with the authors' wishes to alter front-of-house or production arrangements—though as they directed *The Hero Rises Up* themselves, the disagreement that arose about seating and admission was less radical than the embroilment with their director and cast five years later. Since the cautious reticence of Kirbymoorside, John Arden had evidently become capable of making himself felt, and after a heated public discussion during the interval of *The Island of the Mighty*, the Ardens left the Aldwych Theatre, declaring they would 'never write for you again'.

One cannot say exactly how this is to be understood. Arden says he feels himself in any case to be at the end of a phase, so that in various ways this is an appropriate point at which to take a backward look at the twenty years or so of his career. Perhaps because of his conscious professionalism there is a deliberate variation from style to style in successive plays, and apart from the point that the plays about modern society are more broadly comic than the historical plays, categorization is not really possible. Unlike his contemporaries Pinter and Osborne, Arden has never been a professional actor; all the more, then, does he make a point of involving himself in the practicalities of production. Here obviously his collaboration with Margaretta D'Arcy, as well as her participation as actress or director, has been fruitful: the plays published under their joint names, such as *The Royal Pardon* and *The Hero Rises Up*, exploit the theatrical 'situation'—the confrontation of cast and audience—in a way that the non-theatrical, closet dramatist could not achieve. But again, as Margaretta D'Arcy has contributed to many of her husband's other plays, it is not really helpful to regard the jointly published works as a separate group. The most prolific of his contemporaries, Arden has shown that he can use any form or subject, so that, more than his contemporaries, his future development is unpredictable. And unless the Ardens mean never to write for *any* stage again, they may have over half their career yet before them.

II

At intervals John Arden has been compared with Bertolt Brecht. Both playwrights realize their dramatic conflicts in terms of social situations and pressures, rather than in emotional or spiritual developments. But where Brecht sets forth the moral, the 'message' of his plays, however controversial, contradictory or infuriating that moral may seem, Arden's even-handed exposition of motives leaves his audience without even a disputable guideline. By understanding the villains we are tempted to excuse them—they don't seem to be villains after all—and from this derives the difficulty and at the same time the interest of Arden's work.

After the early seafaring drama *The Life of Man*, which, uniquely (for Arden), pits man against the elements, the next few full-length plays, *The Waters of Babylon* (1957), *Live Like Pigs* (1958), and *The Happy Haven* (1960), show his embattled characters struggling against their treacherous environment—though in the latter two the environment is ostensibly benevolent. The Sawneys of *Live Like Pigs* are removed from their tumbledown caravan-shack and rehoused in a new council house. Semi-illiterate and chronically resentful, they have to battle mainly against officialdom—police, doctors, forms to fill in. They are determined to impose their disorganized, tramps' way of life on their unsolicited new house, and officialdom is determined to impose the Council's standards of order, cleanliness and conformity on them. Officialdom as a system is the villain, not because its standards are bad, but because it applies these without imagination or intelligence. Its spokesmen, the doctor, the man from the Council, whether pleasant or unpleasant in themselves, are not responsible for the system as it stands.

The Sawneys themselves live for the moment with terrific gusto, but this living for the moment means that they never clean anything, neither care for the child Sally's sores nor send her to school, and rely on finding something to steal and sell for their beer money. Scavengers on the edge of society, they are however almost respectable compared with Blackmouth, Sally's father. He is a gipsy, racially an 'outsider', totally unsocializable, tottering between spells in gaol —where he has killed to get out—and insane binges. No audience, hearing him howling wolflike round the house throughout the last act, can form the easy conclusion that the Sawneys should imitate Blackmouth as an alternative to social conformity.

Dramatically contrasted with the Sawneys are their next-door neighbours, the Jacksons, who are less enemies than fellow victims. Their vague kindliness overlays an anxiety to keep their nice house, the approval of their neighbours, their sense of security: threatened by the Sawneys' noise and sexuality, they join with other townspeople to attack their house in a collective, uncharacteristic burst of violence which is finally quelled by the police. This time authoritarian order protects the Sawneys.

One of Blackmouth's hangers-on, Croaker, a 'batty old hag', scavenging on the scavengers, is the freest and happiest creature, for all her dirt and madness, in the play. In Arden's next play, The Happy Haven (1960), we see the fate of the 'insiders'—the old people who, unlike the elusive Croaker, have crept or been swept into an old people's 'home' (a cross between a boarding house and a hospital), just as the Sawneys were swept into their council house. Physically cared for, their tastes pampered, these old people have the irresponsibility of children, not only because of their frailty but because of the smothering, paternalistic régime. Carrying this paternalism to fantastic extremes, the doctor in charge of the Haven plans to try out on the patients a rejuvenating potion, an Elixir of Eternal Life that he is secretly developing.

This play, Arden specifies, is intended to be given a formalized presentation, with the use of character masks of the *commedia dell'arte* kind: the purpose is to emphasize the character's 'type' or single ruling trait, so that individual nuances are effaced. The depersonalized, comic old people weave their transparent, self-deceiving intrigues—spying for a sense of power, accumulating money—in a trivial pattern which is suddenly interrupted by a chance discovery of the doctor's experimental intentions. This impersonality gives intense force to the reversal that follows: the prospective patients, at first rejoicing, decide they do not want this further manipulation of their lives, and resolve to stay as they are, to abide by what they have become, to affirm their humanity, one might say. They turn on the doctor, inject him with his own elixir, and take charge of the resulting little boy. This is the positive side of their reaction; there is of course a negative side. Their 'affirmation' is also founded on fear, self-disgust and the envious, sour-grapes persuasions of the only patient to be rejected as unfit for rejuvenation, who tries to steal some of the elixir behind his companions' backs. Experimenting with masks, Arden not only derived practical advantages—the non-realistic convention meant that young actors could be used and a brisk pace was possible —but increased the impact of *The Happy Haven*: the masks underline the stereotyping of the old people as merely 'old' and not at all as 'people'.

The Business of Good Government (1963), Arden's Nativity play for the villagers of Brent Knoll in Somerset, centred on the story of the birth of Christ: the event is presented as simple, unquestioned and miraculous, but is set in a more typically Ardenesque context of tortuous political crosscurrents. A harassed and unhistorically well-meaning King Herod is driven by fear of the occupying Romans to kill thousands of babies who might be the dangerous Christ: the business of good government allows for no miracles, but demands the kind of inhuman logic that treats human beings as objects. Even such an occasional piece as *When is a Door Not a Door* (1958), commissioned to give equal acting opportunities to a class of graduating drama students, makes a virtue of necessity so that the equal status of the characters —the personnel of a factory—becomes the subject of the play, as all, from tea-girl to executive, jockey for more pay, respect or status symbols, while two imperturbable carpenters discuss theoretical politics and mend the door, which is one of the more tangible barriers in the play.

Often the short plays centre on a single experiment that may be used later: the effectiveness of verse was tried in a television play, *Soldier, Soldier* (1957). A soldier returning late from leave arrives in a northern town and tells the family of a missing soldier, Tommy Scuffham, that their son has been jailed for killing his sergeant (in fact, Tommy has been legally discharged and simply disappeared over a year previously). The soldier extorts money from Tommy's parents and seduces his wife Mary, a silent, enigmatic Irish girl. But when Mary suggests that they go and lead a free, wandering life together, he prefers the security—even the punitive security—of the army:

> Here is the Army
> And it's a close house
> And there's square meals a day
> And it's a man's strong life
> Has four measured sides
> Like four forests round one farm,
> And no foul weather except
> Is your own: or a war—
> And we'd be *all* of us in a *war* . . .

Forceful and rhythmic though this is, Arden considered that verse on television was not a resounding success. However, the germ of the conflict, between flexibility and a man's four-square, rigid life, reappears in *Serjeant Musgrave's Dance*, in the central character's pursuit of his duty, which is at once rigid and fanatical. It is 'God's dance on this earth' he says, 'and all that we are is His four strong legs to dance it . . .'

Over a decade after its first production, *Serjeant Musgrave's Dance* is still the play Arden is 'known' for—a classic already well established, frequently performed, a school set text. Its complexity, which initially alienated the theatre critics—it had poor notices and ran for a comparatively short period—is overridden for the more receptive audience by its immediately gripping and powerful dramatic appeal: the colours are a dominating black, white and red, and the plot develops through tense, vivid tableaux, on a twilight canal wharf, in a bright noisy public house, and a snow-covered graveyard. The plot brings four soldiers, scarlet-coated, to a snowbound mining town, sometime in the nineteenth century. Reduced trade and wages have led to a strike-cum-lockout, and the soldiers' arrival is greeted with relief by the local mayor-mineowner, the vicar and the police constable, who hope that a recruiting drive will distract the threatening unrest. It emerges, however, that Serjeant Musgrave and his three men are not really recruiting but 'on the run, in red uniforms, on a black and white coal-field'. This is a play, Arden says, about violence, and these are no ordinary deserters, for the Serjeant's self-imposed mission is to impress on England the sinfulness of the colonial war from which they have come, and the pointlessness of the killing on both sides.

As the preface to the play acknowledges, 'strong' though this plot-line is, audiences felt some residual bewilderment as to where their sympathies were meant to lie. Musgrave's crusade against a 'war of sin and unjust blood' seems at first wholly admirable. His procedure, however, is not clear even to himself. This town is his destination because Billy Hicks, the soldier for whose death the latest reprisals against colonial rebels have been exacted, had come from here, and now he is returning—as a skeleton hidden in a large packing case. The youngest soldier, light-hearted Sparky, has been drawn in as Billy's friend, but as the Serjeant's plot becomes more ominous and more desperate, Sparky's impulse to escape from the whole business appears not cowardice but a sign of sanity. In a scuffle with his comrades, he dies accidentally on a knife held by the pacifist soldier Attercliffe. Musgrave buries the body in a muck-heap, the plan goes on under its own impetus, and the final scene in the market place, starting ostensibly as a recruiting rally, reaches a frenzied climax as Billy's skeleton is hoisted on a lamppost and Musgrave dances his dance beneath it. This is not the final climax, however, for Musgrave proceeds to spell out more explicitly the evil of the colonial war and names the skeleton as Billy, which makes even the most hostile, independent collier Walsh admit the connexion between the distant war and the small English towns that fuel the war with recruits.

The tempo of this long, tense scene is smoothly orchestrated, excitement drops and mounts again, and the apparent anticlimax that follows Walsh's understanding precedes Musgrave's spur-of-the-moment conclusion that he must exact a further twenty-five reprisals for the rebel deaths, and exact them from the town worthies—mayor, vicar, police—who have seemed the most active in promoting local unrest, and warfare abroad. But both Attercliffe and Walsh resist this violence, even *before* the arrival of recruiting dragoons across the thawed countryside. This 'salvation' of the town, with free beer and obligatory rejoicing, is typical of Arden's conclusions, which deliberately give no real solution. Walsh comments: 'We're all friends and neighbours for the rest of today. We're all sold out. We're back where we were.' The last scene shows the surviving Musgrave and Attercliffe in prison, brooding over the ashes of their high endeavour.

Multiplying the ambiguity are the disparate motives of the soldiers—Musgrave's fanaticism, Sparky's personal impulsiveness, Attercliffe's pacifism, and the violence of Hurst, the killer—a violence he imposes, like a fatality, on the 'dance'. Among the civilians, Walsh's caution and independence ends ineffectually, and the only victor seems to be the sly hunchback Joe Bludgeon, ugly personification of opportunism and betrayal.

Arden advises the audience to pay particular attention to Attercliffe and the women characters—Mrs Hitchcock, landlady of the town's best public house, and Annie her barmaid, abandoned sweetheart of Billy Hicks, half daft and 'whore to the soldiers'. It is with Annie that Sparky plans to escape from the Serjeant's inflexible demands, and in the final prison scene Mrs Hitchcock tells Musgrave that his proud adherence to duty, to 'logic', has been a simplification —his favourite phrase is 'That's not material'—and an unnatural one: the disaster was caused by imposing this simplification on the natural, infinitely complicated lives of the townspeople, so that irrational, incalculable elements like Annie's emotions and Walsh's suspicion upset the premises of military logic. Musgrave's arbitrary procedures are part of the war which he is opposing: 'To end it by its own rules', concludes Attercliffe, 'no bloody good.' After the stark contrast of black, white and scarlet, the play closes with Attercliffe's ballad about the soldier's wife who prefers a lover who gives her good apples.

III

Other historical plays, equally sombre in conclusion, were to follow *Serjeant Musgrave's Dance*, and in keeping with Arden's early interest in the medieval, these (with the exception of *The Hero Rises Up*) are set in successively earlier periods: but, concurrently, Arden was writing modern comedies on the lines of *Live Like Pigs*. The earliest, *The Waters of Babylon* (1957), works up to a comic catastrophe, though the death of its central character marks its final curtain. The reference of the title is to the Biblical exile who sat down and wept, and in London, the modern Babylon, exile is shared by the hero, Sigismanfred Krankiewitz or Krank, a melancholy, unprincipled Pole, and his exploited Irish and West Indian tenants—all eighty of them, crammed into his one house. Though determinedly detached and uninvolved in theory, Krank's fate is to be caught up in the passions and violence he tries to avoid, and his practical involvement expands to the point of lunatic farce. Charlie Butterthwaite, a former North-country 'Napoleon of Local Government' whose Napoleonics have evidently ended in disgrace, has been cultivated by Krank, who wants to use his knowledge of local government controls on overcrowding, providing sanitation and regulating the use of premises—all of which Krank is defying with his rack-renting and brothel-keeping. However, blackmail by Paul, a creditor and fellow Pole, who intends to make a large bomb in Krank's house, means that Butterthwaite is set instead on devising a fast money-making plan to relieve Krank of blackmailer and bomb.

Krank's principle is to be without principles: it emerges that his wartime sojourn in a concentration camp was not as a prisoner but as a German soldier where, still a parasite and scavenger, his duties were to black the officers' boots. He then determined never to get involved in any 'causes', and he turns on his violently idealistic compatriot Paul to accuse men of high principle, fervour and honour of causing misery, war and atrocities themselves. Unfortunately, Krank's attempt to be without 'time, place or purposes' is foiled by circumstances, as his different *personae* multiply alarmingly— he is a lodging-house keeper only by night, and by day a respected, dark-suited architect's assistant. Again, to further Butterthwaite's inspiration, a Council-sponsored lottery, he figures as a businessman Alfred Cash. Instead of slipping easily from one *persona* to another, Krank is caught in self-contradiction, and, at last, in the uproar as the plot to 'win' the lottery money goes hopelessly wrong, he is literally caught in the cross-fire between rival nationalists, and stops a bullet meant by Paul for an opposing fanatic. Where Serjeant Musgrave was to die for a cause, Krank dies for an anti-cause, though again the survivors make the conclusion festive, as Butterthwaite leads them in a dialect song about hiding in the cellar from law and order: a lonely and in-effectual programme, as Krank found.

The irrepressible vitality of the characters, always out-stripping expectation, is too much for Paul's simple, violent gestures, as it is for Krank's determined detachment, and Arden never lets his creatures win control over life—like an offended Greek deity, life smacks back unexpectedly. The centrifugal, explosive development of *The Waters of Babylon* forces this lesson on the audience—the anarchic *crescendo* is beyond rational control.

Krank appears again at an earlier stage of his career in the television play *Wet Fish* (1967), though here farce never blossoms on the 'straight situation comedy' (as Arden rather bitterly designates it). Arden had hoped to experiment with visual (televisual) techniques, but the producer preferred his own methods and did not co-operate. Krank is still doubling his architectural and brothel-keeping careers, but it is his boss Gilbert Garnish, a successful, bustling wheeler-dealer of an architect, who now has too many irons in the fire. Like many of Arden's more stately figures, he thinks that with organization and common sense he can manage an unwieldy empire of interests. His downfall follows his underestimation of the emotional involvement, pride and integrity of Mr Treddlehoyle the fishmonger. This character had once been his first client, but Gilbert delegates his building plans to a new, incompetent girl assistant, Ruth. Treddlehoyle takes Gilbert's detachment and perfunctory explanations as a personal betrayal, and when he makes a scene at a business lunch, he loses Gilbert his most valuable clients and forces him to recognize tardily the strong feelings he has aroused.

The strong feelings aroused in *The Workhouse Donkey* (1963) threaten the social and governmental structure of a Yorkshire town in which one of Garnish's disaffected clients, the rich and respected Sir Harold Sweetman, is a major figure. Another is Charlie Butterthwaite, whose hey-day and downfall as a Napoleon of local government is one of the principal features of this play. Nine times mayor, at present alderman, born in the workhouse, he is devoid of tact, gentility or modesty, a deficiency which Lady Sweetman sees as his fatal flaw—'such outrageous vulgarity must be there for a purpose'. This vulgarity he uses expertly as a publicity gimmick in his political career. Sweetman and Butterthwaite head the opposing parties in the council chamber, respectively Tory and Labour. Unscrupulous jockeying for position on both sides is impartially presented, snobbery balances philistinism, and practical policies are apparently much the same: when an outsider, Dr Blomax's daughter Wellesley, asks if Butterthwaite's party misgoverns the town so badly, her admirer, Sweetman's son, answers, 'Oh, it's not exactly misgoverned. It's just the wrong lot are the governors, that's all.'

The catalyst in this play is another outsider, the newly appointed Chief of the police force, the incorruptible, impartial, dispassionate Colonel Feng. Each side would like to use him against the other, and he follows up information laid against both: Butterthwaite and his friends are caught in their habitual drinking in public houses after legal closing time, and the dining and strip-tease club, the Copacabana, used by the richer townspeople and probably owned by

Sweetman, is also investigated. Although these investigations are rendered harmless by Feng's less dispassionate, indeed rather corrupt subordinate, Wiper, Butterthwaite interprets Feng's actions as a personal attack, and with mounting paranoia, ferrets frantically around for scandals to force Feng's resignation. Much of the rest of what Arden calls the labyrinthine and intractable material deals with these scandals, particularly with the Copacabana club, its seductive manageress Gloria, and her incriminating association with Police Superintendent Wiper.

Butterthwaite's feud with Feng is in fact illusory. Feng is certainly not furthering Sweetman's political ends, but is caught up in his own professional treadmill of preserving peace by force. Like Krank in *The Waters of Babylon*, Feng is given restrained, bleak, verse speeches to define himself against the other emotional, unpredictable characters, and in his painfully reasoned soliloquy he notes how the watchfulness and repressive powers of the police cut them off from the people: 'They fear us while they look to us for strength'. (Butterthwaite puts it in a less lapidary style: 'Eh, the Police Force: we can't do without 'em, but by God how we hate 'em.') Within his own personality the necessity for remaining impartial has led to suppression of social and emotional tendencies, an untenable state ironically pointed in the immediately following scene when Feng almost absent-mindedly declares his love for Wellesley Blomax. This lapse into humanity confuses him later in trying not to favour Wellesley's shady father, and ultimately provokes him to resign. Corrupt humanity, his own and other people's, is too much for his logic and duty, as it was for Serjeant Musgrave.

If Feng ends by struggling with himself, Butterthwaite's wounds are equally self-inflicted: the Napoleon of Local Government meets his Waterloo through the reluctant intrigues of cynical, unethical Dr Wellington Blomax. Like Krank, Blomax has his finger in too many pies, and his confidence that 'if it ever gets too hot I can pull out my hand . . .' is misplaced. A liking for secret power makes him establish a financial hold over Butterthwaite, and his slightly illegal professional past gives the Sweetmans a hold over him, so that they use him as a tool to persecute Butter-thwaite. Blomax is swept helplessly by his victim into condoning a robbery, loses his nerve, reverts to the Sweetmans and confesses—then, wavering yet again, distributes publicly a statement revealing plots, counter-plots, bribery and corruption on both sides. Because this is a comedy these misdemeanours seem to cancel each other out, and the party leaders in the final scene lick their wounds and decide that the general scandal has left them ritually cleansed.

The only victim, scapegoat and belaboured donkey is Butterthwaite. Indeed, he is a victim of his own Dionysiac energy. Instead of keeping within the rules of the political and social game, admitting himself unable to pay his debts to Blomax and withdrawing disgraced for a token period, he turns to the wild and criminal expedient of robbing the town hall safe, aided by the temporarily mesmerized Blomax. And when threatened with exposure, cast off by his harder-headed and harder-hearted fellow councillors, he assembles a horde of drunks from the town slums and marches at their head to Sweetman's new Art Gallery, to revenge himself on respectable society by rioting and plundering. Of course his anarchic, turbulent, powerful horde is quelled by the organized policemen, though not before their social superiors have been amazed and frightened at this upsurge. Butterthwaite himself gets into the gallery and, before he is carried out, he sings his final song sitting on the gallery table, swathed in a tablecloth with a wreath of flowers on his head, symbol of the rise of the underdog, the Lord of Misrule.

The play is consciously reminiscent of Greek comedy, and the sudden engagement of Wellesley to young Sweet-man, in another of Arden's ironically inadequate conclu-sions, is as traditional as Aristophanes' final ritual marriages —and as perfunctory.

In the slow unravelling of the plot the main centres of interest have been Butterthwaite and Feng, and to some extent Blomax—each grappling in their own way with a life that rebels against their control. The men set off the plot with a big bang; Wellesley, as the woman in the background, opposes to this a steady state. Like many of Arden's women characters, her attitudes, assumptions and behaviour form a virtually plotless sub-plot, a counterpoint to the more frenetic action. She rejects the uncompromising Feng for the pleasantly average young Sweetman, 'because I don't have to respect you'.

The same decision is made by the wife in *Ars Longa, Vita Brevis* (1963), a very short piece written in the same year. The husband, an art master at a preparatory school, is a parody of rigid characters like Musgrave and Feng, and dreams of the brutal strictness of army life, forbids free, curvilinear drawing, and drills his pupils like soldiers for a new art of straight lines and formal patterns. He becomes an embarrassment to the school, and during an outdoor exercise is shot by the headmaster, ostensibly in mistake for a deer. His wife weeps for his death, but turns naturally to a sensual life of young men and fast cars. Straight lines are not for her: 'I prefer the quick and easy swimming of the fishes', she says, which 'have not a straight line in the whole of their bodies'.

IV

The role of the women characters, eclipsed in the Krank-Butterthwaite modern comedies, was important, as we have seen, in *Serjeant Musgrave's Dance*, forerunner of the series of panoramic historical plays in which feminine values, such as they appeared in *Musgrave*, become more crucial in balancing the argument of the plays. It is interesting to see the difference in this respect between *Armstrong's Last Goodnight* and the earlier *Ironhand* (1963), an adaptation of Goethe's *Goetz von Berlichingen*, in which therefore Arden had less freedom with plot and character.

Since he is a playwright who presents conflicting motives fairly, Arden does not create the type of dominating central character who pushes the others into second place. Not unexpectedly, then, finding that Goethe's hero Goetz monopolizes interest and sympathy, he builds up the importance of Goetz's opponent, Weislingen. Goetz, a frank, independent 'Free Knight' of fifteenth-century Germany, whose artificial metal hand gives the play its title, follows a simple code of feud and friendship (and makes an income by unashamedly plundering his enemies). This code is anachronistic in a medieval society of sophisticated, intriguing rival princes and potentates, a society that has assimilated Goetz's childhood friend Weislingen. When Weislingen is captured—as the right hand man of Goetz's current enemy, a powerful Bishop—he is tempted to join Goetz's robust, uncomplicated life. The women characters here, as in Goethe's original, simply represent the two opposed ways of life. Goetz's beautiful, convent-bred sister Maria will marry Weislingen if he joins her brother; the Bishop's unprincipled mistress Adelheid seduces Weislingen from his oaths and betrothal, and, marrying him, tethers him once more to the court system.

Into this historical picture of a healthy, brutal simplicity being superseded by corrupt civilization, there erupts the mob of rebellious peasants, bent on destroying both archaic and refined societies, burning and murdering without chivalry, diplomacy or religious scruples. More finally and more tragically than in *The Workhouse Donkey*, this uprising of the outsiders is put down by the Emperor's army led by Weislingen. Goetz, who, attacked and dispossessed himself, has helped the peasants—only to be rejected when he tries to impose a code of honourable warfare on the seething, savage hordes—is imprisoned and barely escapes hanging. Weislingen is poisoned by his wife, she is denounced by Maria, and as Goetz dies in prison, a defeated and bewildered old man, he claims the right of human beings to know the real questions of life and asserts their right to answer them. Maria adds their duty to learn from experience. All the factional conflict has been fought as if on Matthew Arnold's darkling plain, 'where ignorant armies clash by night'.

Several of the elements of *Ironhand* were used in new relationships in *Armstrong's Last Goodnight*, the action of which is set on the border between Scotland and England in the early sixteenth century. This wild area was as medieval as Germany had been a century before, and Arden establishes a sense of otherness, of particular and alien conditions, by using a semi-archaic mode of speech which incorporates many obsolete Scottish words and structures. This is at first difficult for the audience, but in the end the unfamiliar idiom not only creates a purposeful distancing effect, but contributes enormously to the forcefulness of the dialogue.

Like the enchantit quern that boils red-herring broo . . . In the pot. On the fire. All the warm sliden fishes, Johnny, out of the deep of the sea, guttit and filletit and weel-rubbit with sharp onion and the rasp of black pepper.

The Lady's earthy sexuality described here is as suited to the brusque directness of the idiom as the courtiers' oratory, which draws dignity from its ancient formality.

The title character, Johnny Armstrong, is as simple, proud and ingenuous as Goetz, but less chivalrous. His position as a boisterous Scottish chieftain or laird of the border is similar to Goetz's free knighthood (except that Armstrong has an overlord and protector) in that his wealth comes largely from plundering the English; this proves a source of embarrassment to a projected peace between the two hostile kingdoms.

As Weislingen's equivalent, Arden takes a historical figure, the poet Sir David Lindsay, tutor to the young King James V of Scotland. His aim is to tame Armstrong for the king by diplomacy, avoiding open or secret violence which creates more problems than it solves. He uses the image of the Gordian Knot, but despises the legendary solution, according to which Alexander made no attempt to unravel the knot, but merely slashed it through with his sword: 'He thocht he was ane god, walken,' says Lindsay, 'Why in God's Name could he no be a human man instead and sit down and unravel it.'

Not only is Armstrong protected by overlords who are stronger than the king, but he is bound by ties of kinship, obligation and brute force to other border lairds—his cousin Eliot of Stobs is one—whose plundering confederacy he is not free to leave. During Lindsay's first attempt at unravelling the situation, Armstrong accepts his bribe—a lieutenantship from the king—and continues exactly as before, re-naming his plundering 'ane just reprisal for enormity'.

Not discouraged, Lindsay begins again; and if Goetz and Weislingen had followed the patterns laid down by their society too blindly, the same cannot be said of Lindsay, who comes up with the astoundingly original project of a 'free border state', as an independent buffer between the two kingdoms, with Armstrong as its chief or president. However, this inspiration is stillborn, for Lindsay finds Armstrong's household vigorously following the directions of a Lutheran Evangelist preacher. Religious enthusiasm is however a specious cover for their unchanged purposes, to extend Christ's Kingdom 'whilkever direction can ensure me the best wealth and food for my people'. Disconcerted by this turn of events, Lindsay owns himself defeated, when his friend and secretary McGlass is stabbed by the Evangelist in a spiritual and mental crisis. Lindsay has dismissed Armstrong's feud-killing of Wamphray as unimportant—'not material' as Musgrave would have it—but now he has to take the killing into account, and after all the diplomacy and circuits, Armstrong meets a summary end. Politely invited to hunt with the king, Armstrong is disarmed and hanged on the spot.

Superficially, the message of the play would seem to be that liberal idealism must always bow to stern necessity, and that violence must be used to end violence—or is it that simple men who trust their superiors will always be betrayed by turncoat politicians? Of course the representatives of idealism and brute force are both ambiguous figures: Armstrong's engaging *naïveté* does not save him from being a brutal boor, and Lindsay's poetry and humanism is flawed by a fatal lack of 'high seriousness'. McGlass accuses him: 'Ye can never accept the gravity of ane other man's violence'. Ironhand had been warned by Martin Luther that 'God cannot abide complexity', and his disciple the Evangelist tells Lindsay, 'The Lord our God is never moderate.' Redirecting the fate of serious, determined men, and possibly redirecting the precedents, customs and destiny of a whole society, is not to be undertaken lightly as an intellectual game, but demands a dedication that perhaps is not within Lindsay's power. So the former violent customs are re-affirmed in the solution that is no solution:

there will be nae war with England: this year. There will be but small turbulence upon the Border: this year. And what we hae done is no likely to be forgotten: this year, the neist year, and mony year after that.

Perhaps Lindsay's inspired political solution was never feasible. Inflexibility and repression pervade this society through and through: Meg Elliot, Armstrong's kinswoman, seduced and abandoned by Wamphray, then driven mad by witnessing his murder, is a victim of the code of war and honour, as was Annie in *Serjeant Musgrave*. The essentially military feudal system breeds its own readiness for violence; only the Lady, Lindsay's mistress, maintains her independence, and though she takes Armstrong too as her lover, she has no intention of thereby serving Lindsay's politics. 'She hath her ain honour', her maid says of her, and it consists in ignoring social rewards and punishments.

The themes of *Armstrong* appear again, insistently, in *The Island of the Mighty*, nearly ten years later. In the interval Arden had been writing mainly shorter pieces and works for small professional or amateur companies. The first of the few full-length, professionally produced plays of this period, is *Left-Handed Liberty* (1965), commissioned by the Corporation of the City of London to commemorate the 750th anniversary of the signing of the Magna Carta. On the whole, Arden's play shows that this Great Charter was not as momentous an enactment of the rights of man, the principles of justice and equality, and so on, as tradition would have it. A product of the bitter power struggle between King John and his barons in the early thirteenth century, the Charter was intended originally to benefit one side or the other in this struggle, and only later was it widely cited as the source of justice for the common man. This capacity for different and usually beneficial applications, beyond the narrow purposes of its projectors, this very fluidity, becomes the Charter's prime virtue in *Left-Handed Liberty*.

However, the flexible, vital nature of the Magna Carta remains largely putative in the play. One of its most lively, amusing scenes shows the wife of John's chief opponent, de Vesci, taxing her husband with beating her—contrary to the provisions of the Charter; and in another, John himself apportions unorthodox justice between a goldsmith, his erring wife and her lover, a priest, much in the manner of Brecht's judge Azdak, so that each gets what makes him happy rather than his legal deserts. The moral is like Brecht's —that this is the ideal, humane, adaptive justice that the Charter should aspire towards. But the rest of the play remains firmly anchored to the Charter's selfish origins, and scenes of logic-chopping argument are interspersed with displays of strength. 'A thoroughly masculine piece of work was Magna Carta—a collaborative effort between brutal military aristocrats and virgin clergy', is how John describes it in a long speech, a scene in itself, addressed directly to the audience. This scene is less illuminating and thought-provoking than might be imagined, probably because of the very similar expository tone of the rest of the play: there seems no reason why John's arguments with archbishop or barons should not have been expressed as audience-directed speech, and vice versa.

The subject of the address is the organic, even miraculous nature of man—all that is ignored in the power struggle. To illustrate what military and clergy are forgetting, John uses Lady de Vesci as a lay-figure—both as beautiful, fickle woman, and as an incalculable human being. But this gallant effort to make a virtue of necessity and point out how Lady de Vesci and her concerns have been ignored does not really compensate for this deficiency in the plot. 'The Lady is peripheral', says John—as the ladies were peripheral, not material, in *Musgrave* and *Armstrong*. But Lady de Vesci lacks even the tragic relevance of Annie and Meg.

Earlier, Arden had isolated this eternal, symbolic opposition of human freedom and social bonds in *The True History of Squire Jonathan and his Unfortunate Treasure* (1963), a mythical story of a freedom-loving lady and the bonds of economic dependence. In his Grimm's-fairy-tale castle, Squire Jonathan, a wretched, ugly, nervous, brooding little man gloats over his chest of sumptuous, use-less treasure, fearing the Dark Men in the forest outside and dreaming of a large white woman. But when such a woman in fact arrives, is persuaded to take off her wet clothes, and permit herself to be adorned with his treasure, Jonathan is suddenly seized with suspicion, hostility, and fear of finally realizing his dreams. The outraged beauty breaks open her own chastity belt, flings off the jewels and leaps out of the window into the arms of the dirty, rough but carefree Dark Men. The indolent, generous and generously-built damsel, 'a great, blonde, milky woman, a giantess', has no time for the small meanness of Jonathan, walled about not only by his ancestral towers but by his dependence on his unproductive treasure. Naturally she throws in her lot with the Dark Men, who have no possessions.

However, in Arden's next long play, the large lady and her small lover are happier in each other's affections. An exception among the historical dramas, which have tended to move steadily back in time from *Serjeant Musgrave's Dance*, *The Hero Rises Up* (1968) returns to the nineteenth century, to the story of Admiral Nelson and his mistress Lady Hamilton. George Bernard Shaw, writing on Ireland, had taken Wellington and Nelson as typical respectively of the down-to-earth English and imaginative Irish temperaments: to the Ardens, too, Nelson is of a Celtic 'asymmetrical curvilinear temperament to an unusually passionate degree'. When the intuitive, passionate Nelson channels his energies into the inappropriate career of naval warfare, the result is extraordinary butchery: he was the first commander to understand 'the entire and total destruction of the enemy fleet at whatever cost to my own'. Feverish, undisciplined energy harnessed to a crude, brutal system does not moderate the brutality but makes it worse. It is, however, Nelson's natural gusto that attracts him to Lady Hamilton, a big and beautiful whore whose acting talents and exceptional good luck have transferred her from mistress of an officer to wife of his uncle, Sir William Hamilton— the old, impotent ambassador at Naples, where she meets Nelson. Predictably, after Nelson's death and contrary to his wishes, the British government bestows large sums of money on all his family, including his estranged wife, but nothing to Lady Hamilton. Energy, it is felt, should mainly be confined to the (naval) job in hand. The fiction of good order and organization is realized in the most flagrant of Arden's ironically artificial conclusions: the final scene takes the form of a musical tableau of Nelson's apotheosis. Supported by both wife and mistress, he rises up in a marine chariot 'reminiscent of the popular twopence-coloured prints of Nelson's own day'—gaudy but two dimensional. The commentary meanwhile marks the sad moral that accompanied *Serjeant Musgrave's Dance* and its final jollification:

> Equality, Fraternity, and so on never came:
> And where we were then, now we are just the same.

This is the admiring crowd's own fault: 'he did what we required', and they have the hero they deserve, both in that his genius was harnessed to no better ends and in that they never tried 'to do without him on our own'. Nelson here stands for all heroes, all great leaders; and much to his disgust the more peaceable Emma compares him to Napoleon in needing to batten on slaughter.

However, *The Hero Rises Up* is again an exception among the historical plays in sustaining a savagely comic tone throughout: the naval and revolutionary bloodshed is grimly and grotesquely caricatured (the King of Naples's gruesome sadism, for example), and Nelson's heroic characteristics are farcically deflated. His premonition of death, his last prayer for victory, are at once labelled 'blood and molasses' by his hostile stepson, and the sailors comment with disillusion—what choice have they got, they ask—on the famous message, 'England expects that every man will do his duty'. Altogether, the play is very different from its predecessor, the rather static *Left-Handed Liberty*, particularly in its visual 'busyness', the continual dancing and singing (no question here, as befell *Live Like Pigs*, of the songs getting pushed out of the action), and the frequent heated escalation of the scenes—as when a frenzied party accelerates into a book-burning orgy.

In the Preface to *The Workhouse Donkey*, Arden had wistfully suggested the possibility of a 'promenade play', where the audience (armed with synopses) could circulate among separate little stages viewing different scenes at will; and with *The Hero Rises Up*, directed by the dramatist and his wife, now again his collaborator, at the Roundhouse (a huge, circular, former engine-shed in London), the Ardens returned to this concept. They wanted to write a play that does not have to be 'done properly'. In this case, the single thrust-stage as set up was not suitable for radical departures in audience arrangement (though since then plays *have* been produced there in this multiple, promenade style). The Ardens' other ambitions for the play, such as free admittance, brought them into conflict with their backers, the Institute of Contemporary Arts, and though the production went forward, the later published preface comments that theatre practitioners—actors and writers—are coerced as much by the Scylla of public subsidy as by the Charybdis of commercial saleability. This opinion was to prove an obtrusive bone of contention in the Ardens' next play, *The Island of the Mighty* (credited as by 'John Arden with Margaretta D'Arcy').

This last work is said to deal with the relationship of the poet to his society, but already in the sixties Arden was taking theatre and the writer as subjects for plays. *The Royal Pardon* (1966), written by John Arden and Margaretta D'Arcy for children and performed by amateurs in Beaford, Devon, shows a company of travelling actors evading a vindictive comic policeman, who in the end finds that 'the force of anarchy wins all the time'. The play is subtitled 'The Soldier who became an Actor', and Arden's later 'Autobiographical Play', *The Bagman: or, the Impromptu of Muswell Hill*, might have been subtitled 'The Playwright who became a Soldier' for in a dream the Narrator (playwright) is transported with his sackful of tiny wooded actors to a barbaric, rich town, living parasitically on burien treasure. He is involved in the underground resistance of the thin Outlanders, who are brutally kept from the townspeople's prosperity, but resists the rebel's cry that drama is irrelevant to real fighting, and that he must wield a common sword with the rest of them. The Narrator wakes, still clutching his bag; but Arden's preface, added after his experiences in India had made him more militant, states that this attitude is 'reprehensible, cowardly, and not to be imitated'.

V

In *The Island of the Mighty* (1973) most of the themes of Arden's earlier works have been united in the many-stranded plot: a survey of the play is a survey of Arden's drama in little. Again, the role of the hero is questioned, and an alternative title might be 'The Hero Sinks Down'. A panoramic history of the legendary Arthur's final years, its grim humour and tragedy are a long way from the lurid satire of its predecessor. Originally written as a trilogy, and reduced to a roughly tripartite unity, the action is set in the Britain of the Dark Ages after the Romans have left, and its Arthur—not a king but a Roman-style general—is an old man trying to protect the country against the invading Anglo-Saxons or English. For Arthur and his countrymen are Celts, though (being Romanized) not as 'asymmetrical, curvilinear' as they might be. Arthur himself is a straight-forward, determined, insensitive (but not stupid) warrior, undefeated for twelve battles, destined to know defeat in his thirteenth. There are hardly any traces of the traditional Arthurian legends here—no Sir Lancelot, no Round Table, no Holy Grail—but Arden's creation of an Arthurian Britain has just as much authority. Arthur's efforts to pull the dissident petty kings and princes of Britain together to face the common enemy are in vain; already the land has lost its peaceful Roman identity, trampled into barrenness by local feuding war bands.

The hopelessness of this war-oriented society is illus-trated in the fate of twin brothers, whose story is framed by Arthur's organization of his defences. When their family is killed in an English raid, the more aggressive of the brothers, Balin, leaves his twin in anger to take service under Arthur against the English. Impulsive and tactless, he sees no reason why Arthur should seek to conciliate the matriarchal Picts or Cat-people, who are threatening an inopportune war against one of his British allies. Superior force can settle them, thinks Balin, and kills the Cat-people's ambassadress (thus cutting the Gordian knot, as Lindsay would say). Apart from being a sacrilege, this action involves Arthur in the delay and expense of a war against the Picts, and Balin is dismissed as a troublemaker. He then creates equal havoc at his next port of call, the palace of the devious, pious King Pellam, who, while pretending to arm against the English, secretly aspires to overthrow Arthur.

Because Balin is more concerned to protect the bondswoman whom he has rescued from her outlaw protector Garlon (and whom he thinks of marrying) than to worship Pellam's holy relic, a full-scale brawl ensues. The bondswoman has implored Balin to forget the treadmill of vengeance, to forget fighting, and join with outcasts such as Garlon (also called Cain and Barabbas), in a free community. Like Lindsay's free border state, this dream is unrealized, and the bondswoman is killed during the brawl. Despairing, and tired of violence, Balin embarks for Ireland. Meanwhile his twin Balan has fallen in with the Picts, whose rulers are all women but who all participate, men and women alike, in battle. After fighting for them, Balan is caught up in a different kind of ritual violence: chosen by the Princess, he kills their king, and is ceremonially lamed. The brothers, who had determined to order their fates in different ways, are brought to a common end by the tide of war: Balin is shipwrecked on the Pictish shores, captured and set to fight his twin. Both are masked, and unknowingly kill one another. The only hope offered in this grim adventure is that the Cat-people, appalled and kingless at the unprecedented loss of both contenders, guess that their Goddess wishes them to abandon this savage custom.

Emblematically, this plot within a play mirrors the fate of Arthur's larger-scale operations. He too is a lame ruler, eventually killed by a kinsman. In the middle part of the play he marries Gwenhwyvar, a beautiful, dangerous young widow, reputed to have killed her first husband. He quells impertinent behaviour on her part by force, and for the time being Gwenhwyvar is left to regret the legendary days of the Daughters of Branwen—yet more of Arden's 'huge ladies'—who inhabited the country in a golden age of agriculture and food-gathering, a matriarchy unlike that of the militaristic Cat-people. Meanwhile, dissension about tactics simmers between Arthur and his lieutenant (and supposed nephew) Medraut, as troops are massed by defenders and invaders. Gwenhwyvar is told by Morgan, Arthur's old, outlawed sister and a reputed witch, that she is a direct descendant of Branwen, queen of the huge ladies, though her mother has died before teaching her the secret powers of her position. At once fired as much by a wish for revenge on Arthur as by a sense of her destiny, Gwenhwyvar chooses Medraut as her consort and he, intoxicated by her urgency and by the sudden enthusiasm of the people, always latently pagan, turns his army against Arthur, whose outdated strategy seems an obstacle to victory over the Anglo-Saxons. But the result is the mutual extermination of both British forces, the triumphant invaders pouring in to seize the undefended country.

Obviously the women characters in *The Island of the Mighty* have a role that is crucial in the plot—whereas in the earlier plays it is usually possible to describe the plot first, and the significance of the women afterwards, peripherally, which could be said to *be* their significance. And indeed here Gwenhwyvar's activity is far from promoting the life and love that Mrs Hitchcock in *Serjeant Musgrave* defended. Like the Picts, she is indoctrinated by a warrior civilization, and makes a disastrous choice in Medraut, who is simply a younger, handsomer version of Arthur. But if many of the women have abandoned life and love in any real sense, the poets in the play, who are neither subordinate like the women nor warriors like the other men, are theoretically dedicated to poetry, freedom and the peaceable arts. One poet is attached to every court as verse-maker and diplomat, much as was Sir David Lindsay. In practice, they have mostly been absorbed into the warrior system too: Taliesin, the Duke of Strathclyde's poet, is an old, conventional courtier, fond of his creature comforts; Aneurin, poet to Gwenhwyvar's impoverished brother, is the freest—a rebellious, disrespectful, thoroughly unmilitary young man; but the major poet is, of course, Arthur's Merlin. He acts as narrator to the play, linking the changes of scene from kingdom to petty kingdom, moving rapidly over the island in person in his role as ambassador, trying to make counsels of reason prevail, trying at least to cobble up a general amnesty that will further Arthur's defence against the English. And over the years his poetic feeling, his integrity, has become subordinate to Arthur's policies. His young wife Gwenddydd has left him fifteen years earlier for this reason, to reappear later as Gwenhwyvar's companion-confidante.

It is Merlin's usual rationality, and his particular relationship with the audience as narrator, that makes his tragic error so shocking: just before the battle between Arthur and Medraut, he refuses to perform the poet's duty of trying to reconcile the armies. He wants Arthur to inflict a decisive, crushing defeat on his rebellious countrymen. It is left to the old, hobbling, ridiculous Taliesin to toil backwards and forwards between the two camps—and almost, by virtue of his authority and desperation, to succeed. But, as the armies stand, awed into inaction by Taliesin's last appeal, Merlin himself takes a spear and strikes down the sacred, unarmed poet-ambassador. Taliesin falls, cursing his attacker; Merlin flees, distraught and insane; and the armies begin their mutual slaughter.

The last part of the play, which was greatly compressed in performance, deals with the fate of Merlin and the way the survivors' lives go on after the invasion—not a falsely glorious, victorious conclusion this time, but a realistic anti-climax. Arthur and Medraut have been killed, Gwenhwyvar has disappeared—captive, we are told, to an undistinguished Anglo-Saxon. Merlin is living naked in the trees of a weird, Strindbergian Glen of the Madmen, fighting with the other madmen for his share of the watercress that grows there. As he says, 'I used to stand aside . . . now I take part'. Reluctantly, Aneurin undertakes to lure him back to the remnants of Arthur's court, as Gwenddydd is being held hostage there. But Merlin has passed through a suffering that has purged all his policy from him: he is no use to courtiers or warriors now, and he escapes to run over the mountains with Morgan, his first love, a Daughter of Branwen and, in a way, goddess of freedom. However, a poet only lives through his audience and after Morgan's death Merlin follows a little community of peasant Britons, as much in search of a listener as of food. This community is ruled by Taliesin, who has recovered, renounced worldliness, and become a repressively pious Christian priest to his flock. He wishes to reclaim Merlin too, but his former colleague is saved from new spiritual bondage: he is killed by the jealous husband of the woman who feeds him.

Only Aneurin has refused to compromise, and his survival proves not too painful. He sets up house with Gwenddydd, becomes a blacksmith's assistant, and makes his poetry in his spare time. So he brings an individual peace and stability to his own household, but not, as would have been the case had Gwenhwyvar chosen him instead of Medraut, to the whole kingdom.

To appreciate the richness of this play makes greater demands upon the audience even than Arden's earlier works simply because the plot, as in *The Workhouse Donkey*, proliferates majestically. A second viewing or reading is really necessary to interpret the relationships of characters or groups of characters, and the unspoken dramatic contrasts and symbolism is important—for example the lameness of the Picts' sacred king and of Arthur. Similarly, we note that the bondswoman eats a green apple which reminds Pellam of the unregenerate Eve, but reminds us that the apple was set against the soldiers' blood-red rose in *Serjeant Musgrave*. However, with a cast including so many poets, Arden's early problems about juxtaposing verse and prose are aptly solved.

Arden, then, considers that he has now reached the end of a phase. If so, *The Island of the Mighty* ends that phase with a bang, not a whimper. However, concurrently with this play the Ardens were putting on at the shoestring Bush Theatre a modern, topical play, *The Ballygombeen Bequest* (1973), dealing with a case of wrongful eviction of a tenant in Ireland, a case known to the Ardens personally. This action became the subject of legal dispute, and the play had to be abruptly taken off. So perhaps the phase ends, with Ardenesque ambivalence, with a whimper as well as a bang.

Finally, looking back to the fifties and *Serjeant Musgrave*, it is clear how John Arden's dramatic powers have been, not changed, but enriched by experience—especially by the strongly visual contribution of Margaretta D'Arcy's collaboration. A playwright of the preceding generation, John Whiting, said: 'I think everybody writes one play on which he then draws technically for the rest of his life. You have on paper a sort of anthology of what you can do'. If *The Island of the Mighty* gathers most of Arden's themes and techniques into one mighty plot, *Serjeant Musgrave's Dance* is that first, economical blueprint, and the line between the two plays is a direct one. Whether *Serjeant Musgrave* will still be the blueprint for the next phase remains to be seen.

JOHN ARDEN
A Select Bibliography

(Place of publication London unless stated otherwise)

Collections:

THREE PLAYS (1964)
—contains *The Waters of Babylon*, *Live Like Pigs*, and *The Happy Haven*.

SOLDIER, SOLDIER, AND OTHER PLAYS (1967)
—includes *Wet Fish*, *When is a Door not a Door?*, and *Friday's Hiding*.

TWO AUTOBIOGRAPHICAL PLAYS (1971)
—*The True History of Squire Jonathan and his Unfortunate Treasure* and *The Bagman; or, The Impromptu of Muswell Hill.*

Separate Works:

SERJEANT MUSGRAVE'S DANCE: An Unhistorical Parable (1960).

LIVE LIKE PIGS (1961)
—in *New English Dramatists*, 3.

THE HAPPY HAVEN (1962)
—in *New English Dramatists*, 4. Written in collaboration with Margaretta D'Arcy.

THE BUSINESS OF GOOD GOVERNMENT: A Christmas Play (1963)
—with Margaretta D'Arcy.

THE WORKHOUSE DONKEY: A vulgar melo-drama (1964).

ARMSTRONG'S LAST GOODNIGHT: An Exercise in Diplomacy (1965).

ARS LONGA, VITA BREVIS (1965)
—with Margaretta D'Arcy.

IRONHAND (1965)
—adapted from Goethe's play *Goetz von Berlichingen*.

LEFT-HANDED LIBERTY: A Play about Magna Carta (1965).

THE ROYAL PARDON; Or, The Soldier who became an Actor (1967)
—with Margaretta D'Arcy.

THE HERO RISES UP (1969)
—with Margaretta D'Arcy.

THE BALLYGOMBEEN BEQUEST, *Scripts* 9 (New York), September 1972
—with Margaretta D'Arcy.

THE ISLAND OF THE MIGHTY (1974)
—with Margaretta D'Arcy.

Critical Studies:

CONTEMPORARY THEATRE, ed. J. Russell Brown and B. Harris (1962)
—Stratford-upon-Avon Studies IV. Includes a chapter 'Realism and Parables: From Brecht to Arden', by G. W. Brandt.

ANGER AND AFTER, by J. Russell Taylor (1962)
—revised edition, 1969. Includes a chapter 'Presented at Court: John Arden'.

'Kirbymoorside '63, with a footnote by John Arden', by I. Watson, *Encore*, X, vi, 1963, 17–21.

'Producing Arden: An interview with Tom Milne', by W. Gaskill, *Encore*, XII, v, 1965, 20–6.

'Arden's stagecraft', by A. Hunt, *Encore*, XII, v, 1965, 9–12.

'Arden: Professionals and amateurs', by A. Hunt and G. Reeves, *Encore*, XII, v, 1965, 27–36.

THE ENCORE READER, ed. C. Marowitz [and others] (1965)
—contains '*The Workhouse Donkey*', by C. Marowitz, and 'The Hidden face of violence', by T. Milne.

DRAMA IN THE SIXTIES: Form and interpretations, by L. Kitchin (1966)
—includes a chapter 'Epic as drama: Arden'.

'The Motives of pacifists', by M. Page, *Drama Survey*, VI, 1967, 66–73.

JOHN ARDEN, by R. Hayman (1968)
—in the 'Contemporary Dramatists' series.

'John Arden's use of the stage', by J. B. Tindale, *Modern Drama*, XI, 1968, 306–16.

'Love and anarchy in *Serjeant Musgrave's Dance*', by J. Mills, *Drama Survey*, VII, 1969, 45–51.

'John Arden and the public stage', by S. Shrapnel, *Cambridge Quarterly*, IV, 1969, 225–36.

'Political progress of a paralyzed Liberal: The Community dramas of John Arden', by S. Trussler, *Tulane Drama Review*, XIII, iv, 1969, 181–91.

'*The Island of the Mighty:* An interview with David Jones', *Plays and Players*, February 1973.

JOHN ARDEN, by S. Trussler; New York (1973)
—Columbia Essays on Modern Writers, No. 65.

ARDEN: A Study of his work, by A. Hunt (1974).

WRITERS AND THEIR WORK

CHRISTOPHER SMART: G. Grigson
SMOLLETT: Laurence Brander
STEELE, ADDISON: A. R. Humphreys
STERNE: D. W. Jefferson
SWIFT: J. Middleton Murry
SIR JOHN VANBRUGH: Bernard Harris
HORACE WALPOLE: Hugh Honour

Nineteenth Century:
MATTHEW ARNOLD: Kenneth Allott
JANE AUSTEN: S. Townsend Warner
BAGEHOT: N. St John-Stevas
THE BRONTËS I: & II:
　　　　　　Winifred Gérin
BROWNING: John Bryson
E. B. BROWNING: Alethea Hayter
SAMUEL BUTLER: G. D. H. Cole
BYRON: I, II & III: Bernard Blackstone
CARLYLE: David Gascoyne
LEWIS CARROLL: Derek Hudson
COLERIDGE: Kathleen Raine
CREEVEY & GREVILLE: J. Richardson
DE QUINCEY: Hugh Sykes Davies
DICKENS: K. J. Fielding
　EARLY NOVELS: T. Blount
　LATER NOVELS: B. Hardy
DISRAELI: Paul Bloomfield
GEORGE ELIOT: Lettice Cooper
FERRIER & GALT: W. M. Parker
FITZGERALD: Joanna Richardson
ELIZABETH GASKELL: Miriam Allott
GISSING: A. C. Ward
THOMAS HARDY: R. A. Scott-James
　　　　　　and C. Day Lewis
HAZLITT: J. B. Priestley
HOOD: Laurence Brander
G. M. HOPKINS: Geoffrey Grigson
T. H. HUXLEY: William Irvine
KEATS: Edmund Blunden
LAMB: Edmund Blunden
LANDOR: G. Rostrevor Hamilton
EDWARD LEAR: Joanna Richardson
MACAULAY: G. R. Potter
MEREDITH: Phyllis Bartlett
JOHN STUART MILL: M. Cranston
WILLIAM MORRIS: P. Henderson
NEWMAN: J. M. Cameron
PATER: Ian Fletcher
PEACOCK: J. I. M. Stewart
ROSSETTI: Oswald Doughty
CHRISTINA ROSSETTI: G. Battiscombe

RUSKIN: Peter Quennell
SIR WALTER SCOTT: Ian Jack
SHELLEY: G. M. Matthews
SOUTHEY: Geoffrey Carnall
LESLIE STEPHEN: Phyllis Grosskurth
R. L. STEVENSON: G. B. Stern
SWINBURNE: Ian Fletcher
TENNYSON: B. C. Southam
THACKERAY: Laurence Brander
FRANCIS THOMPSON: P. Butter
TROLLOPE: Hugh Sykes Davies
OSCAR WILDE: James Laver
WORDSWORTH: Helen Darbishire

Twentieth Century:
CHINUA ACHEBE: A. Ravenscroft
JOHN ARDEN: Glenda Leeming
W. H. AUDEN: Richard Hoggart
SAMUEL BECKETT: J. J. Mayoux
HILAIRE BELLOC: Renée Haynes
ARNOLD BENNETT: F. Swinnerton
JOHN BETJEMAN: John Press
EDMUND BLUNDEN: Alex M. Hardie
ROBERT BRIDGES: J. Sparrow
ANTHONY BURGESS: Carol M. Dix
ROY CAMPBELL: David Wright
JOYCE CAREY: Walter Allen
G. K. CHESTERTON: C. Hollis
WINSTON CHURCHILL: John Connell
R. G. COLLINGWOOD: E. W. F. Tomlin
I. COMPTON-BURNETT:
　　　　　　R. Glynn Grylls
JOSEPH CONRAD: Oliver Warner
WALTER DE LA MARE: K. Hopkins
NORMAN DOUGLAS: Ian Greenlees
LAWRENCE DURRELL: G. S. Fraser
T. S. ELIOT: M. C. Bradbrook
T. S. ELIOT: The Making of
　'The Waste Land': M. C. Bradbrook
FIRBANK & BETJEMAN: J. Brooke
FORD MADOX FORD: Kenneth Young
E. M. FORSTER: Rex Warner
CHRISTOPHER FRY: Derek Stanford
JOHN GALSWORTHY: R. H. Mottram
ROBERT GRAVES: M. Seymour-Smith
GRAHAM GREENE: Francis Wyndham
L. P. HARTLEY: Paul Bloomfield
A. E. HOUSMAN: Ian Scott-Kilvert
TED HUGHES: Keith Sagar
ALDOUS HUXLEY: Jocelyn Brooke
HENRY JAMES: Michael Swan